to kim   my partner   my collaborator   this book would not exist without you

to all those who have supported me   you are always welcome

to my readers   this book is combustible   please treat it with care

"We are humus, not homo, not Anthropos; we are compost, not posthuman"

-Donna Haraway, *Staying with the Trouble: Making Kin in the Chthulucene*

table of contents

not
hum
an
eno
ugh
for
the
cen
sus

[the creature of dark habits]

          is whispering an echo to my other face
that I created
    so that the creature would have someone to finger

the way I move my eyebrows is a mask of feathers
that the creature's fingers pull through
         my body my face's body
             my
         fingerbody

many times at night I look into the creature and slide
        under the pillow
        like a feathered toad

yes we are closer
than your eyes
flicker the shutter against our bodies
if you want to capture the

        time

            when tethers were needed to restrain the body
      from dying in
      its own skin   which stuttered   its goosebumps
                  all over
        the damn house
creating a mess   that I fingered up
with a paper finger a finger
that I cut
out from an origami flower
with a stem that went on forever

which ends up amounting to the number of hairs that are on the stomach of a
tick
whose legs crick against the shadow
created by my tethered teeth
you see
they don't want me to bite anymore
because
my signature is too familiar for any lab
because
I was born I was born I was borne
a child who is a finger
whose body is a hangnail
who knows at least 3 math problems
right out of the womb
the most important being
anything times 0 is 0
and therefore he bites his hangnail
down to the cuticle
so people call him fleshboy
they call him cute little icicle
they call him if they need money
blow
cigarettes
a good time
a slice of ham
another excuse
for not being
quite human
enough
for the
census

[nightmare chorus]

there is a nightmare growing inside you and sometimes you wake to the sound of a rat gnawing at the glass of your nightmare and your nightmare is wearing a papier-mâché mask of your nightmare who is also there cooing like a dove nightmare with a flask nightmare whose last name is nightmare and who lives down the block from your lung capacity which is not enough to hold your screams when you knock on every door nightmare

wear our skins for coats in the netherworld
and unicorns sip our essence from their horns
which are the garnish of the future because
let's face it
the only future is fiction
and the present is only
      a panel of three
      that decides our fate
      as a species

[once there was a tree]

only one tree because the world had ended already
    (it was nuclear war
    it was the nuclear charge of the nuclear body
    that shot its dust into the sun
        it was the climate that never stayed static
        but whatdoyouknow
        actually burned way too hot one day
        because all the bees died
          because
            of our nuclear honeymoon
            because of our
            swigging of honey
            because we never
            gave a shit
            about bodies
            that did not
            walk
            upright)

the world had ended
and the last body alive
had to produce bodies
so it produced a whole colony of bees
                              from its ears nose and throat
                    and not before it had produced a flower from its spine
                              (an orchid I believe)
                              and that's not before a new sun had blossomed from
                              its lips
                              and not before
                                             its body itself became that tree
                                             that one last tree
                                                            as its feet
                                             rooted
                                                            into the ground
                                             and eyebrows sprouted
                                             leaves that were more
                                             voluptuous and hairy
                                             than any leaf you have
                                             ever seen before
                                             and then these leaves
                                             produced a whole
                                             population of slugs
                                             and worms and apples
                                             and pears and also a lot
                                             of tiny woodmites

and then of course
    me
    at 36
    I came last and
I am
        not a
    voice
        not a
    word
        not a
        larynx
        not a
        squirrel
        I am
        that
        which
        opens
when you knock it
that which is forever
36
until
I am only a memory of
ash

[the marsh inside became willow]

and spilled
          from my mouth
                              in a sweep

now the tree that grows
between my teeth
is an infinitely splitting atom
with delusions of grandeur

[atom and weave]

were banished
                    from my bowels
in the year of the squirrels

god is a walnut
that I stowed away
for the winter
but the shell
            would never crack

now this tree in my mouth
pulses
through me
trying to create its adam
its skip hop and believe

[god is liquid in the tempest]

of carbon atoms that
        split
and chatter
        pattern upon
the sky that was just a stain of blood

toothbright inside
insight into the molecular spattern of light
grotesque aftersin

calculate the velocity
of all those bodies
that stagger so swiftly
to the tune of an openwide satisfied stutter to the stagger of

breatht
rick

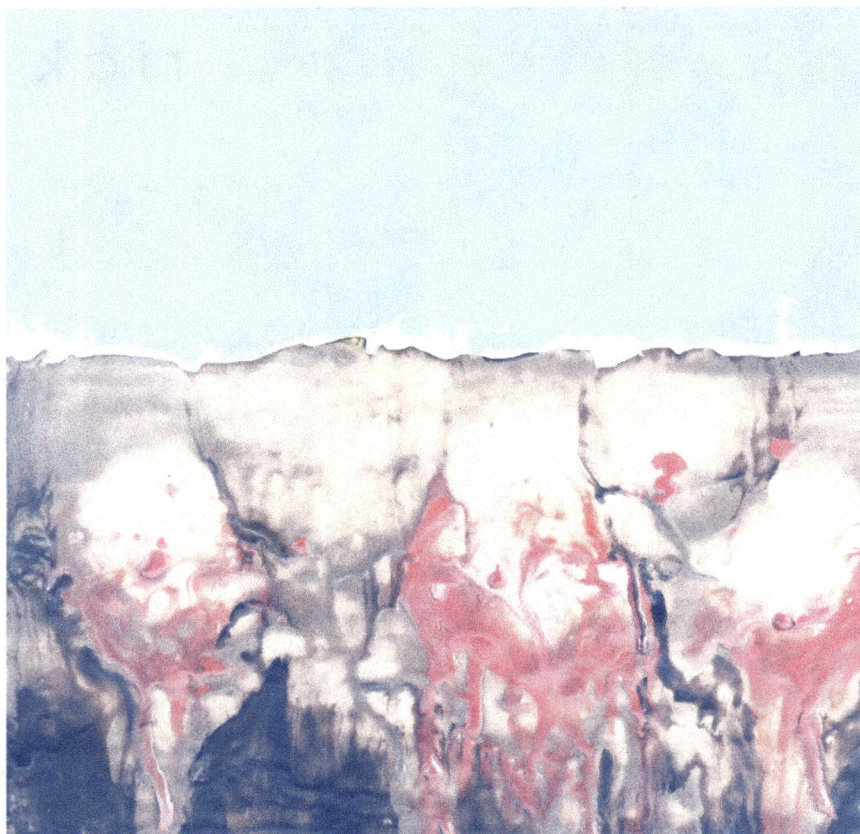

                        dustfather
mothmother   merged
in my heart   that dark webbringer
        awful spider in my bone
                catacomb
                crawling
                        tick tick legs
                                tick tick
                                        none

I want to   I want
        who I
I am kneaded clay

                no shape   no memory
                        I have   lost you
        who   I have
                not you
                        dark shoe
                                untied
                                blue ribbon

come to me
                rabbitsfoot
come to me
       through
            soft bone   crack

       thump thump
               bang

       burning
           turning
               come

hello   I am   breathdust
*   a seashell   broken in*
*   your mouth   I am*
*   an angel   with no wings*
*   burnt flowers and ash*

dear mr death
        dear mr love
            where are you now   and who
                tick tock
                        tick stop

                            hello   I am
                                        your friend
                                        lover
                            broken by your whip
                                        shift   shift
                                                snap

                            burnt flower ash
                            burnt angel
                                    I am I am

31

come to me
           I am broken
      come to me
           I am waiting

*   do I   do I*
find you very dark
*   very sad hook   caught in the mouth*
*   of the world*

*   taste me bread-child   I am silk in*
*   the throat*
*   I am the presence of all that is absent*
*   let me fill you*
*   let me return the dust to your body*
*   the moth to your heart*

dustfather

        mothmother
    clay ash pit

        I will
             tear you
             from the roots
             of that sick tree
                       black at the throat
        I will

the fruit of sorrow is red   fuller than moon
its skin tough as an eyelid and warm

if you eat of it you will see everything holy
angels trembling wings of gold burning

like newborn stars

m
e
h
t
n
a
h
c
a
o
r
k
c
o
c

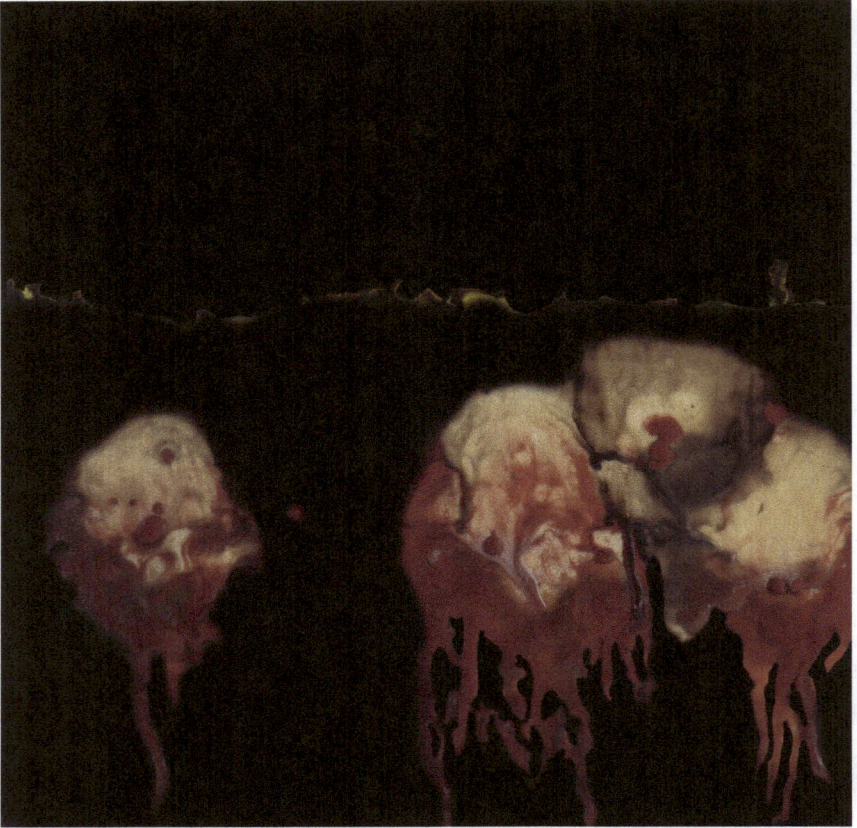

[the organ breathers]

the organ breeders took a day off to be organ breathers because there was a typo on the memo that day and they were bred to be literal so they took a deep breath and pressed their lips against the cold skin of a cirrhotic liver which miraculously sputtered and spit as they exhaled and life spilled from its ocher body

triumphantly the organ breathers continued blowing their life into the liver's puckered flesh in slow steady streams

once it blushed they placed it in the body of a young mare which instantly revived and bucked its mane in joy

[simple toxins]

                    secreted by
        invertebrate skin cells
                            matriculate in bloodurine
        your body
                    is hemmorageswing

temporary solution:
shut
            your pores
        to the sound   of wail belly
                                            scrub
                    your lipcrossed
            ligaments
                                    in the cicadic night

[in my innerdrum: a chlorine blight]

from you I learned a lean body
a traipse of longing across the yard
when seashells stormed
overhead
without any moisture:
a sponge of darkness swathing the sky

[an indication that there are not enough fracked fissures]

a whole mile of hole
                    will extend the life
          of an imaginary body
                              a body
                                    that's scribbled
        with holes
                        without lungs
                        without breath
                        without body   a fraction
                              of the fissured frack
        a snap
              in the weight
                            of naphthalene
              a squatter of matter
                                  tipping the splatter
to the surface

[shroom destructioom]

a tree felled
in the fellshroon
couple of swoons with an oiled
tune-
    cluck uck ck k

— — —

throat is cuzzy
        huzzy
            uck
                ck
            cluck

—

mushwoom in the thicket
mudbloom
ashmush breathing through
the silo with a sigh
        low
            cuffing fit

darlingguzzleleanintomyglut

there's no escaping these mudclots in the bloodsplean

[a chainwinked spider]

                    in the swipe of
                              glittering
                slips
      the wire
            onto my body
   as I
                sling
                        the cockroach anthem
to the wind

[lab report]

under consideration:
     gills
     tracheas
     s. freud's left molar
     whale droppings

the answer is not:
     crab teeth
     owl pincers
it does not include the universe
the answer has the heart of a black hole
leave it the fuck alone

there will be

solitary confinement
                                for the correct answer

[perhaps fine unpopular mice]

ingest a human genome
                        result:
                        prodigious impersonal death
             such as:
                        molecular stopp
                              age

(int/er?lud!!e)

[speaking light protests,]

earlier this/ month ?explain? coming   apart _freedom_inequality of meaning *overture smile* wide magical inside bury now that jewel hiding thing love wide opening (.) war speeds turning need shine

        SHOESHINE: $20 Dollars
        THROATCUT: -7% for those with bonus points
?
        ?\
    ?

a scar swept under ligament laundry

                        [spackle blood tainting the ground where the body freckled the
                pavemen]t

a weather rhythm dan   ces its static like a stut   tered throatSong

   stuttttttttttt   ered   SoNg

time took water QUICK?er
     #forsake the water sound *overflow stones*
beasts left to rust >down<
   pocket stones sucking in order (00001 1 01 01110_) of the e/u/c/h/a/r/i/st the body bro<ken into pockets that *rattle* the waterbones

    WATTTTTERRRRRBONING: Sell your SOLE (...)

light freedom heat matter BLOOMWALLSTONE

(Christ and Bloom in the bathertub flowering in the rub the tub the sins forgiven yes are they yes are they are they-----------

the wailing willow shattered blue masochistic confession

        ERROR 666: ?breathwriting?

diaphanous scriptorium a dozen %tiny wings% bat ting the echoes of eyelids

the alley where those rats are [gnawing] stones that used to be eyeballs hard shells
that were once a jelly confession

     ^that alleys are sourcream swilling stations blacklung borders /built according to code stray
from the stench and anIIIhilation licks out its flickering flower *thorned* like the hand of the
___devil___ who is just a cockroach fantasy

  a thousand c/l/i/c/k/i/n/g fibers sewn across the landscape thunder is NoT welcome here
because all the static eLeCtRiCiTy has been swallowed and is now w/h/i/r/r/i/n/g within tiny war
machines with

     ?mouths like swans mouths which aren't mouths which are beaked peaked
pecked   removed and displayed on the
            WATERTABLE:

is thinning into thighs that trickle skin across the oceanfloor while the rats yes the rats they are
the sovereign they are the diseased they are the bodies which don't stop moving when they aren't
wound they are the ones that are handing everyone else tickets to the rapture in which rat teeth
will click and legs will tick tick tick tick tick tick tick tick tick

  "Agamben wonders what is a tick like when it is not tick"like when "it i"s not
heatSeeking   and bloodLetting when it is sit/
         ting for decades with a dormant #hunger with a reminder of a distant tickness that
has been evacuated by time's
      "tick tick tick tick tick tick ti"ck""

the claws are stubbled&scuttled&scorched&reminders of the body that simmered shimmering
stones a lot of stones weigh down the world gathering all used spines left overs from a time when
time was

jeweled words Cutt ttt ttting

thres

\

holds

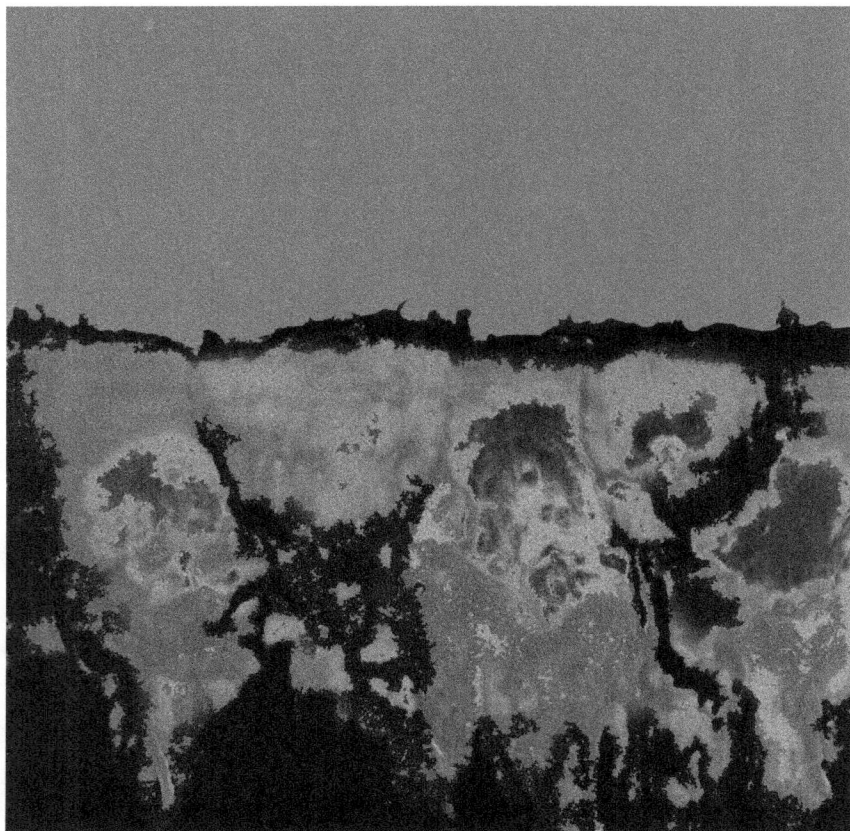

[thresholds]

his hat made him look like an armadillo in a rainstorm but he swore it was a swan song made from his final sweat a knitted masterpiece tucked beneath his ears that would usher in his demise as a human and resurrection as the world's most realistic mannequin

his friends were surprised that he ever considered himself human in the first place

[all filiation is imaginary]

                    confession: my dog is not my son
                         he is too good looking

all filiation is imaginary:
        I have no
                         father
                               not becoming
                                                father
        becoming fish
                gilled heart
                gilded tongue
                a spider RANSACKING
the
        web
of
        my throat

                         tick suck spatter

is the devil a louse a rat a fly
can a louse take witness

I think I left the hollows of my eyes in my becoming
                              fruitfly
                                   scorpion
                                        sinkant

dear universe
my dog told me to ask you for my father's bones that you carry on your back
                                    sisyphus
                                    chicken little
                                    mother mary full of bloat

love
the mailman

love
I am

love
fill in name here

[bullet goose]

there was a goose who lived in my grandmother's attic

it had lived there since the first world war and had bullets in its flesh where feathers once grew and its daily clickaclink rang in our ears each morning as it dragged its cyborg body across the unfinished floor

every now and then it would bury its face in the pink insulation so as to shield its beak from our eyes because it was graying and wrinkled and come to think of it not very gooselike at all

[the eyes are wider than the mouth]

but the mouth
is the width of a moth standing on a coinpurse
because the mouth
is angry
and is itself pursed and
          a breath of greymatter just escaped the brain
          and went to a party hosted by the great gatsby
                    (who actually turned out to just be ok
                    but) had great scarves the color of lemon ice or orange Julius
                    or a baboon's buttocks
                    which is so red that it deserves its own color zipcode: 1111RED
                    where you will find the anthropologist scratching
                                        his head
                                        at the way his hands
                                        have become shovels
                                        and his legs
                                                  become stars
                                        because he has found
                                        the key
                                        to a world
                                        where objects are not quite
                                        what they seem in car mirrors
                                        but instead are smaller
                                        than pins buried in haystacks
                                        where little blue boy
                                        gets higher than a kite on
                                        Ambien

[stagger into
        the horse's body]

                where god is but a shell swaying
        on an esophagus of neighing
                                don't worry no horses were harmed in this poem
                                        only embodied
                                        only recognized as a body
                                        worth being a body
                                        that is not just for the whip
                                        or for labor
                                        but for pleasure
                                        for understanding for spiritual growth
                                        read a fucking handbook whydontchya
and you will understand
that these hooves are made for walking
in that the horses in Connemara are more beautiful
        than your stupid soul can ever be because
        it is soaked in the dust that god created you from
                                how did god create the horse from light
                                                from cloth
                                                from the sun
                                                from clay from
                                                NEIGHboring
                                                worlds
                                        you know those in
                                        which you are an alien
                                        and those little green
                                        men
                                        are just plain people
                                        laughing at your stupid
                                        looking head and your
                                        strange little bodies
                                        which can't even break
                                        the speed of sweat

[wolves wrestling shovels]

from their mouths
moths flustering flickers of dogstooth
jammed
against the transmission of that thing called love
which you caress every yesterday with a pair of hands borrowed
from the shelf of a priest who lopped off a limb
every tuesday for contrition
for ammunition for a day
when he could walk on water without any feet
and multiply fishes using only his tongue
which is in a glass jar next to his teeth
next to his piano forte
continuously playing bach's brandenburg concerto number 3

I only play on the left side of the piano
because I have blacklung
and I am a flitter in the ashtray
                a whimper in a glass
                            a hollow stutter in the windowpane
                            a gutted body of a fish
                            a swift swipe of light on the subfloor
                            with its large crack in the foundation
                                            make sure you put on some rouge
                                            so at least the disaster
                                            is a beautiful disaster
                                                    a volcano exploding
                                                    with glistening lips

[my body a weight]

tied to a neck
who tried
to feed itself
by the stars
          a bizarre
replication   of that time you panicked
me into lopping limbs
                  you remember:
that cattleshocked
          shadowfleshed
                  humpbacked
showdown
                  of clear white ice

                  only to watch bones
sharpen like swordfish
slide out of life on the ten thousand smooth stones
I have swallowed
to survive
sinking
into
oblivion
squatting
tightly
to the beat
of the bottom of my nightmares
where the seedy sallow stench of bodies smokes

body count

[pleasure body]

will heft itself
on thistles   pock
its skin in the soft places
draw enough
blood for a blur
of pleasurepain
and then make itself a warm salve
of leaves and green tea.

       pleasure body knows how
       to breathe
       just shallow enough
       to create heartbeats
       feels the heat
       expand
       from skin to bone
       when a hand
       is placed
       on the stovetop

when pleasure body has time
       it traces itself
              on the walls
              streets
              stadium
              sky
              feels itself swell   with light

[8 millimeter body]

                                    doesn't understand that NRA stands for
                                                never
                                                        returning
                                                                again
                    after an open   gunshot   wound
                                            to the head
                                            or the heart
                                            or the parts of the body
                                            where flesh yields to
                                            bone yields to sky

[petroleum body]

remembers
the first time it tasted
        oil
                slugged
                down
                the throat
                and
                clogged
                its lungs

                the pipeline that ran
                through the world
                had cracked
                        and coughed up
                        oil
                        into the bloodstreams
                                via throatpipes

[gasoline body]

wanted water
so badly
it went right
to the sourcepipe

but thick
          was the color
          of salvation
          that day

          one could see gasoline
          body's breath congealing
          at the moment of contact
                         as if the breath had become an object
                         something one put in one's pocket
                                          shimmering

there is still a shape lodged
in the dirt from the day
that gasoline body hit
the pavement
and pain
          fracked
                    a scream
                    from the throat
                    in the shape of an olive
                    that gasoline body now keeps
                    under its pillow
                    to feed its nightmares

[the floodwaters come]

leave or you
will be the cause
of your own
deaths
you've had due warning

a bedridden body
closes
its eyes

   shuddaleft they scream

         a body with no wheels
         just feet
         and a dozen cans of campbells
         creates a makeshift
         pantry in its bathroom medicine cabinet

               must not care about their lives they taunt

               prisonbodies crouch
               in their cells
               used to being left behind

[1 in 100 scientists agree]

that liquid
is the state
of god
      a shapeshifter
with a whole lot of wrath
says the pearltoothed preacher body high on swigs of holy water

                        a slumped turnip body
                        with a labcoat
                        nodding behind him

when the floodwaters rise
bodies
are caught in this liquid
god's feverdream
        the church on high
        is their only salvation
        but the preacher body
            is too busy
            praying at its altar
            that it forgets
            about the other bodies
            nobody can disturb his holy body when it is a praying body

bodies pound and knock
pleading sanctuary
to the locked church doors until
their fists deaden the thunderwind
and they become liquid
            slip
    through the cracks in the door
        that their fists make
            become themselves the god
                of destruction
                  and sweep
              the olive branch
              from the altar
                      as they rush the pulpit

[some important white
man once said]

       "those were the pearls
              that were his eyes"
though many eyes
are slowly
filling with oil
           as water thieves into superfund sites in houston
           reminding the world
           of its dirty
           little secrets
but some bodies have always been haunted
their houses built on toxic remains
their bodies breathing in
the dust of industry's buried bones
lead in the stomachs of bodies in flint
oil in blood
breastmilk
saliva
of those whose bodies
will never become pearls
      who were gifted
      coal eyes
      as pearl bodies ate
      oysters in the sky

[I knew
          I could deal with this]

     I

         can deal with this
               it is only one less
                      body   one
                      more absence

            I can handle absence if it comes
                  in ones
                  if it comes
                  by itself
                          wrapped in tears   weeping

              just dry it out:

                      it is no problem
                      it is no mess
                      only one less thing to hold
                      only one less body to remember

            if they keep it coming
                one by one   if they keep
                    dying with the turn of the clock
                        tick tick tick
                        if they keep moving backward
        into death
                      in a forward motion
    if they
    keep
    coming
    as individual
    bodies

   I will become a master at this

one by one by one
          the bodies pile up
until one is many
          one
          too
          many

just because the body is gone
does not mean the absence of the body is gone

the tree

but

the butchers

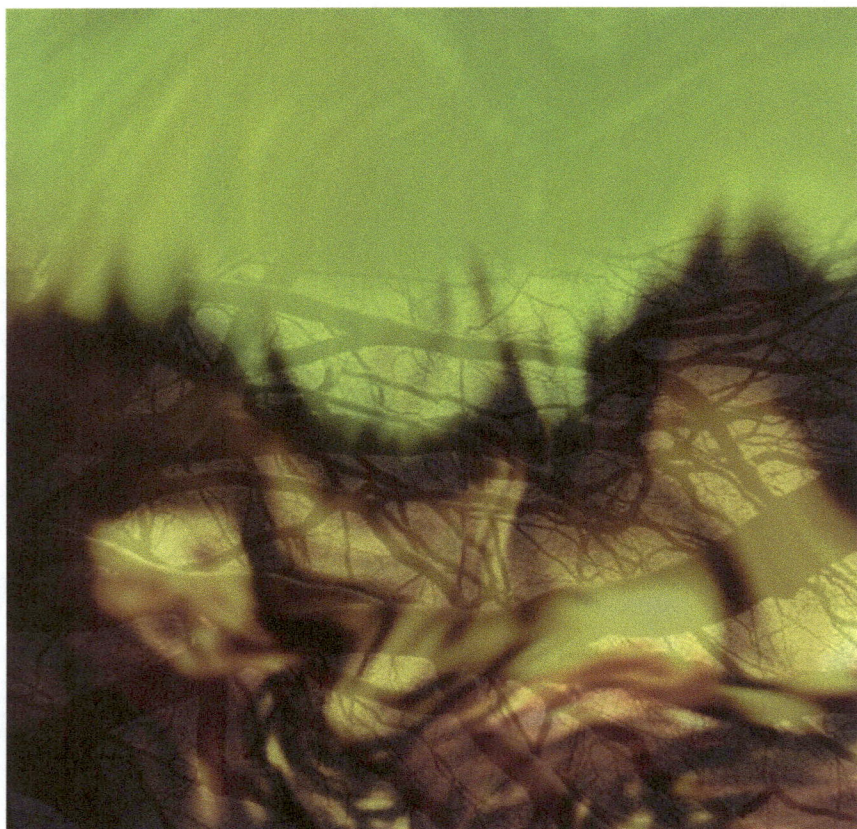

the treebutchers made 20 hits a day

their hands calloused
like the bark   they eat twigs
                  consuming their kills

cannibalism is a thin red line
                  especially when
                  the treebutchers began to sprout
                  leaves from their eyes

the treebutchers read
ionesco's *the rhinoceros*
    as they brush
        the leaves
            out of their line of vision

            though it is hard to read when your entire eye is in the shade

christ is
believed
to have told hypocrites
to *cast out the beam*
from their own eye
before casting the dust
out of their brother's eye

            so the treebutchers begin to blow in each other's eyes
            but the leaves continue to sprout

one of the treebutchers manages
to read Ionesco's entire play
through the side of their eye
and turns into a squirrel

the treebutchers beg it
to clear the leaves
from their eyes
with its teeth but
it climbs a tree instead

            when they cut it down
                    the squirrel bites them
                        in the fingers instead
                          then runs away

the blight
of the treebutchers
infected them each
at a different pace
         some began to root whereas some
            continued to cut

eyes were not needed to butcher
              their bodies had its rhythms in their bloodstreams

soon all the treebutchers took root
and the cutting stopped
                          along with the growing

the treebutchers petrified
and the squirrels bit
off their broken branches
trying to save their homes
in the treebutchers mouths

                    to no avail

.

the apocalypse came as a treebutcher   slicing

                                               down the petrified trees with its teeth

list of images

acknowledgments

I am grateful that versions of several of the poems in this volume were first published in the following journals:

BlazeVox: [the eyes are wider than the mouth], [stagger into the horse's body], [Wolves Wrestling Shovels], [Shroom Destructioom]

Crab Fat Magazine: [body count] (originally published as a prose poem without [pleasure body], [I knew I could deal with this], and [8 millimeter body]) and [8 millimeter body] (originally published as [the man with the 8 millimeter])

Dream Pop Press: [perhaps fine unpopular mice]

EPIZOOTICS!: [all filiation is imaginary]

E·ratio Poetry Journal: [god is liquid in the tempest], [simple toxins], [an indication that there are not enough fracked fissures]

Figroot Press: [there once was a tree]

formercactus: [thresholds]

Microfiction Monday Magazine: [the organ breathers]

Otoliths: [speaking light protests,], [the treebutchers], [pleasure body], and [I knew/ I could deal with this]

Riggwelter Press: [lab report]

SPF Lit Mag: [the creature of dark habits], [breathtrick], [nightmare chorus], [the buffalo]

Unbroken Journal: [bullet goose]

X-Peri: [the marsh inside became willow], [atom and weave], [in my inner eardrum: a chlorine blight], [a chainwinked spider], [my body a weight]

www.ingramcontent.com/pod-product-compliance
Lightning Source LLC
Chambersburg PA
CBHW062151020426
42334CB00020B/2564